is for Hell

A thought-provoking collection of dark, unnerving poetry

LANCE BARNWELL

H

is for Hell

A thought-provoking collection of dark, unnerving poetry

LANCE BARNWELL

MEREO
Cirencester

Mereo Books

1A The Wool Market Dyer Street Cirencester Gloucestershire GL7 2PR
An imprint of Memoirs Publishing www.mereobooks.com

H is for Hell: 978-1-86151-391-5

First published in Great Britain in 2014
by Mereo Books, an imprint of Memoirs Publishing

The address for Memoirs Publishing Group Limited can be found at
www.memoirspublishing.com

The Memoirs Publishing Group Ltd Reg. No. 7834348

The Memoirs Publishing Group supports both The Forest Stewardship Council® (FSC®) and
the PEFC® leading international forest-certification organisations. Our books carrying both the
FSC label and the PEFC® and are printed on FSC®-certified paper. FSC® is the only
forest-certification scheme supported by the leading environmental organisations including
Greenpeace. Our paper procurement policy can be found at
www.memoirspublishing.com/environment

Typeset in 12/18pt Plantin
by Wiltshire Associates Publisher Services Ltd. Printed and bound in Great Britain by
Printondemand-Worldwide, Peterborough PE2 6XD

MIX
Paper from
responsible sources
FSC www.fsc.org   FSC® C004959   PEFC PEFC/16-33-415

Another thought-provoking collection of dark poetry
by Lance Barnwell, author of Dereliction.
Sometimes unnerving, often creepy, but always horrific.

Contents

666

Darkest Demons

666

'Twent so quickly, my insipid sanity
Packed up and left with my vacuous vanity
But I'm sure I'm fine, I have to say
And who needs that baggage anyway?

I know I'm quiet, as I sit here staring
Though not talking my thoughts I'm sharing
But you seem unsure, like I'm a perilous poser
If you want some answers come one step closer

You look perturbed every time I giggle
So I admonish you with a finger wiggle
You can't see the joke, see what's funny
And if you're not laughing you should be walking, sonny

You can stay or go, or run a mile
If you're afraid of my smarmy smile
Who's the enigma with no sense of humour
Is it you or me, or another pneuma?

So where did it go, my insipid sanity?
It left me behind and took my vacuous vanity
But if time exists, it's now that I should begin
To ignore the outer and look within

I gnash my teeth with every single niggle
As the creepy-crawlies make me wriggle
So be on your way, start running, sonny
'Cos there's nothing here remotely funny

'Twent so quickly and now it's hard to think
Packed up and left; left me on the brink
And where you are is where I stood
Before it went and went for good

All my darkest demons stand here staring
Though not speaking dire thoughts they're sharing
And what was once clear, I now can't find
In the tortuous turmoil of my mind

I'm in the grasp of their invisible arms
As they acquaint me with their uncharitable charms
How they can drain my will is quite uncanny
As the creepy-crawlies find every nook and cranny

In my twilight hours, in all the seasons
They're always here, my darkest demons
In their mind-vice grip I start to choke
And now it's me who can't see the joke

I know I'm quiet as I sit here staring
But I've naught to say or thoughts worth sharing
Beneath my sweat and mucus the spiders wriggle
As the creepers crawl I have to giggle

I can feel them feeding as they slowly slink
In the mushy matter where I used to think
They ravenously ransack inside my skull
Till they drain me dry and they're leech-like full

There're spiders, millipedes and fire ants
With screaming banshees and their wailing rants
And my desolate eyes are only focused
On the beating wings of a swarm of locust

All my darkest demons are here for sharing
And might you be next to sit here staring?
You could've run and run, up to a mile
But you chose to stay for just a little while

In the festering wounds of our internal lesions
Is the pernicious presence of our darkest demons
How their infection spreads is quite uncanny
As the creepy-crawlies find every nook and cranny

Let us giggle through our corrupted lips
But the jokes aren't funny, nor are the quips
And how they irk with their relentless prodding
Till we grind our teeth and our heads are nodding

We quiver and shake with insanity's incessant chill
As we take and swallow each bitter pill
But they're still here and giving reasons
Why they'll never leave us, our darkest demons

'Twent so quickly, our insipid sanity
Packed up and left with our vacuous vanity
And I know we're quiet as we sit here staring
But the creepy-crawlies are never sparing.

The Fever
666

I screamed from the dream of the wolves in the wood
They were snapping and snarling and wanting my blood
Come the light of the morn I'll depart with the cleaver
And escape from this bothy that's causing the fever

I slumber by the door on the boards of the bed
My confused rationality is butchered and bled
Through the snow, on the morrow, I'll be forging my track
And not dreaming the dream of the wolves in a pack

By the flames of the fire I am safe, I am sure
I have wedged, I have blocked, I have sealed the door
But with every shift of a draught, or the wind in the branches
Gives the permeating doubt the fuel for advances

They stalk in the shadows, where they fade and they flicker
With a hunger so ravenous that for first bites they bicker
They've the scent of my odour, they'll never let go
Till they're fed to the full and I'm just bones in the snow

From the depths of the wood a secretive howling
Or maybe an owl that's causing my cowering
The night is unyielding with manifestations of dread
And I'm alone in the dark in a glorified shed

I dream of the chase in the thick of the wood
The thrill of the hunt with an adrenaline flood
I take care of one with the blade of the cleaver
Snow bound in this bothy am I suffering the fever?

The grey of the morn seeps through the glass of the pane
I climb from the bed and step on a stain
Dying embers from flames and nerves that are raw
As I trip on my boots that I'd left on the floor

Through the miserly square window still is the snow
In the firs of the wood my fears fester and grow
In the day or the night in this winter world frozen
They'll loiter for gain 'cos I'm the one chosen

I yearn for the comfort of warmth and the crust of a bread
And my reasoning restored, and not the gathering dread
The shifting of timber, the movement of branches
The reservoir of doubt is taking its chances

I feed the fire with the last of the kindling
Then return to the bed with my sanity dwindling
I pull up a sleeve for the flesh to meet cleaver
Snow bound in this bothy I'm bleeding the fever

That what loiters abroad is creeping in snow
And what loiters within is the fear that'll show
I dream of the carnage in the heart of the wood
The ripping and gnawing, the taste of my blood

Drip...drip...drip, I top up the stain
The fever that's burning is killing the pain
Through the square of the window yellow eyes glowing
I smile to myself, they'll not follow where I'm going.

Dominion

666

With false enlightenment we found the path
And raised an army to face the wrath
Then laid siege and stormed the gates
And found beyond our festering fates
What we espied was hard to bear
No hope in dreams or answered prayer
The void of heaven was an empty shell
Long since looted by a horde from hell

Amongst the ruins we searched for plunder
But discovered our presumptuous blunder
No precious metals, oil or cash
Only porous rocks and scattered ash

We sought to seize a perceived dominion
But found abandoned souls of lost opinion
Armed for battle like heroes brave
In a dire semblance of a ravaged grave
With our idle trident and vicious sickle
Not one drop of blood had cause to trickle

So it was we had time to dwell
And chose not to pray or ring a knell

Below the clouds of fibrous cirrus
Adrift in smoke by broken mirrors
No treasure trove of glistening jewels
Only porous rocks and voracious fools

Crestfallen we withdrew through the broken gates
To the loam of home and our festering fates
With our baggage train bereft of swag
We returned to naked fields and hills of slag
Alas heaven fell to the hordes of hell
They ransacked and ruined and left an empty shell
So it came to pass that we gained dominion
Of the abandoned soul of the servile minion.

The Beacon

(Do You Dream of Hell?)

666

I know it's scary, I know it's frightening
The smell of ozone, the flash of lightning
But they're close behind you, the Hell gate keepers
The Candyman, Reaper, the jeepers creepers

Worry not, for you're only dreaming
'Cos I can't hear you fucking screaming
Keep on running, there's a beacon's light
The only refuge in this oppressive night

Run and run hard and don't look back
Suck in the precious air and never slack
'Cos if they catch you they'll cut your throat
And you'll cross the Styx on a burning boat

You'll exist in fire, with no chance of dying
It's no comfort, but I'm not one for lying
Your only hope is that distant beacon
And your resolve that cannot weaken

I know it's scary, the crashing thunder
That shreds your nerves, till they're torn asunder
But they want to meet you, the Hell gate keepers
Hook and scythe, the jeepers creepers

Are you worried, or are you dreaming?
If this was real you'd be fucking screaming
Call to Jesus, he's your pastor
But he'll not help you run any faster

Run and run hard on legs of lead
Your face is strained to the colour red
Can you hear them in the Shades
Moving smoothly with their sharpened blades?

When you're burning there'll be no chance of dying
You may think I'm joking, but I'm not one for lying
Your only hope is that approaching beacon
But you're fatigued, as you start to weaken

I know it's scary, the thunderous lightning
But don't look back, 'cos that's more frightening
You can smell death's odour, on the Hell gate keepers
The Candyman, Reaper, the jeepers creepers

Now start to worry, 'cos you're not dreaming
'Cos I can hear you FUCKING SCREAMING!
You've finally reached the beacon's fire
But it's a writhing mass, a funeral pyre

A boat awaits you upon the oily Styx
The ferryman beckons, as his switchblade flicks
And there's no escape, no dream erasers
They're right behind you, with blades like razors

Scythe-whipped and hooked, throat cut to stop you crying
Then bound to a blazing boat, with no chance of dying
Where's your Jesus pastor, or archdeacon?
As you burn and float from my entrapment beacon.

Hocus Pocus
666

Hocus-pocus Charlie Tan
With his assistant, Madame Shan
No card tricks or fake illusions
His was the magic of self-delusions

Harlequin conjuror, manic eyes hazy
With his chainsaw and blade his act was lazy
No sleight of hand, he had the gift
And a captive audience on a graveyard shift

He heard the voices in a static blizzard
And they assured him he was a wizard!
Charlie Tan with his hocus-pocus
In his final show he lost his focus

The woman in the box was not Madame Shan
But an audience member, as per the plan
In the guillotine a dupe put his head
A minute later the stage was claret red

Chainsaw and blade made such a mess
With bloody entrails over suit and dress
The shock and horror of high-pitched screams
Are found in nightmares and not in dreams

Hocus-pocus Charlie Tan
Ably assisted by Madame Shan
There's no magic in your illusions
Only a static blizzard of self-delusions.

The Ivy Cottage
666

I felt her touch and heard her say
'This old boy is on his way'
A proximate presence of stale breath
And inner whisperings 'This time it's death'

Through a drowning whirlpool I start to wend
I fight the vortex, I try to fend
In ethereal static I'm hearing voices
Someone says 'there's always choices'

With my blinded eyes I can clearly see
A guiding light has been sent for me
I can smell crusty bread and steaming pottage
As I hear the words 'They're in the Ivy Cottage'

In the dappled light of a sunshine beam
I cross the footbridge of a woodland stream
The forever warmth of a day in May
Comforts me as I wend my way

Sombre songbirds are in ivory towers
As I tread a trodden path through lilac flowers
And then I'm there on a ten acre lawn
Burnt by the sun to the colour fawn

In the unseen distance, in his boiler (blue) suit
With a hand he beckons, like a man born mute
And so I approach his cracked tooth smile
Each five steps seem more like a mile

Through the grasping grass I have to wade
As he leans himself upon a Teflon spade
Caught on the breeze a mad dog howls
In the sheltering shadows a quiescent cat scowls

And he greets me with a knowing look
Like I've took the bait; sinker, line and hook
'There's crusty bread and steaming pottage'
He said 'Over there, in the Ivy Cottage'

I see him point and hear him say
'You're much too late, so be on your way'
'I've a hole to dig, now I've caught my breath'
So I ask of him 'Is this the path to death?'

He laughs so hard that he sheds a tear
'I'm just the gardener, who knows not your fear'
'I mow and prune, to my spade nothing sticks'
'Now go to the place of the ivy clad bricks'

With my blinded eyes I can clearly see
A wooden door that's ajar for me
He had said 'Go within and drain your bowl'
'Leave naught to waste, or I'll have your soul'

In the dappled light of a sunshine beam
On a marble plinth, but lacking steam
The bait that brought me is a sight too cruel
Mouldy green bread and putrefied gruel

There's a mortuary fridge with an open door
Inside there's a waxen body with a slackened jaw
I gaze upon the death mask guise
Into the empty pits of my absent eyes

In the unseen distance, in his boiler (blue) suit
With a hand he beckons, like a man born mute
And so I run to his cracked tooth smile
Each five strides seem more like a mile

With my blinded eyes I can clearly see
That the gardener's dug a hole for me
Caught on the breeze a mad dog howls
In the sheltering shadows a quiescent cat scowls

And so he greets me, with that knowing look
'Cos I've took the bait; sinker, line and hook
He says 'There's no crusty bread or steaming pottage'
'There's just your abandoned soul in the Ivy Cottage'

Sombre songbirds are in ivory towers
I'm in my grave, amongst the lilac flowers
He shovels dirt with his Teflon spade
Then nods his head; a farewell made

Through a sickening cesspit I start to wend
I'm blind and soulless and cannot fend
In ethereal static I'm hearing voices
Someone says 'Beware of choices'.

Shadows of the Moon

666

The unfathomable shadows of the menacing Moon
Are impenetrably dark and seemingly hewn
Empty black patches, like burial holes
Wanting to feed on wandering souls

Sable shaded shadows cloak the reapers gallows
Hides the presence of the bone filled barrows
And upon the frozen wastes of a wild moor hill
Draws in the nomadic, like it's the Devil's will
Open fissures of death-slide pits
Wend disparate ways to the rancid Styx
Self-sating vortices, night time feeders
Omnivorously voracious and dead ground breeders
Feel the resonance of the vacuous hollows
Take one step closer and two dry swallows
Heaven can wait, when Hell is calling
Edge one foot closer and feel the force of falling
Menacing moonlight of malevolent hues
Opens the vents of frozen moorland flues
Outside a hamlet's warm comfort aura
No soul is safe amidst the funereal flora

The unfathomable shadows of the menacing Moon
Are impenetrably dark and seemingly hewn
Empty black patches are burial holes
Gorging themselves on wandering souls.

The Ghosts of Marston Moor

666

In twilight storms their fates are sealed
As those long lost roam the blood-soaked field
Felled in battle, they still fight their war
Now vagrant souls, the ghosts of Marston Moor

In the half-light gloom you can almost hear
The meandering wastrels still courting fear
The peasant conscripts and the landed gentry
All butchered here in a foregone century

Shadows thicken amongst the Whitecoats' slaughter
In their wretched death throes they gave no quarter
Now kith and kin lie in a pit of sorrow
A corps of corpses who never reached the morrow

How bitter sweet the full moon shines
On those abject souls cleaved from lines
Formless figures, ripped and torn asunder
The restless dead who are left to wander

No peace in sanctuary, no road home
Forever bound to this foreign loam
Only midnight whisperings borne on the breeze
Of hapless sobbing and hopeless pleas

Lead to slaughter, like ignorant cattle
Those who fell still fight the battle
Thunder rips like a culverins roar
Stirring lost souls, the ghosts of Marston Moor

All Our Gods
666

All our gods are much too violent
They had a lot to say, but now they're silent
They'll not arbitrate to get things sorted
Hold to account; have warlords thwarted
Come and see us, you've had time to muse
Divulge your wisdom and pay your dues

All our gods are our own reflections
And tread the paths of designed directions
They cannot save the meek from dying
In needless conflicts caused by lying
Give us a call, there's no need to hide
And point out to us the righteous side

All our gods support us, them and others
The mean, the mad and the psychotic brothers
But there's no panic here, we can stay calm
Because our god has provided napalm

All our gods are what man desired
Ludicrous lore scribes who all conspired
Left their laws for the sheep-like masses
Of crime and punishment and open clashes
Under the welkin of the vacuous void
Rogues and knaves like a counterfeit Freud
Guide, though ignorant, but have a penchant
Of oppressing free will with a guilty conscience
Dead weight doctrine of attrition
Shackling their cohorts in absurd tradition

All our gods must hate us, one and all
Bloodthirsty tyrants, 'to arms' they call
But they're all transcribed; in our image cast
In the hateful dogma of dark days past

All our gods are word of mouth, then hand written
Pandering to those who are easily smitten
They'll not protect against high tide surges
Or cleanse our souls of perverted urges
Come and see us, let's have a meeting
Your presence lately has been too fleeting

All our gods are much too violent
And forever now have been silent
They can never get things sorted
Hold to account; have warlords thwarted
Give us a call... no, we'll call you
And imprint upon you our points of view.

Hide and Seek
666

'One' he said and got to four
And then you fled through an open door
Rush in hush, hide and seek
Desperate breathing, floorboards creak
Five to twelve brought to tally
You're the hunted prey, no time to dally
Empty corridor, empty room
His ominous voice the clock of doom
'Thirteen... thirteen!' screamed high pitch
'You're gonna die boy, like a witch'

You run for cover damp from drizzle
With a conjured thought of a hammered chisel
'I'll count to thirty' is what he said
'And a short time later you'll be dead'
Fourteen to twenty-one heard too clearly
You're nowhere safe, not close, not nearly
Upstairs, downstairs, which way's best?
To foil the madman's bloodthirsty quest
You tick the tocks and make your choice
And hide away from his doom-laden voice
Up to twenty-seven and then there's silence
The last few moments before the violence
In the dark you count the thirty
Hot and sweaty, scared and dirty
Only hush with hide and seek
Silent footfalls, floorboards creak
'Thirty' shouted 'you'll convulse and twitch'
'Then I'll dump your body in a ditch'
One minute, two minutes absolute max
He's leisurely followed the drips of your tracks

You came in from the murk of the drizzle
And found him with his hammer and chisel
'Hello boy' he said 'let's play a game'
'You don't know me, but you know my name'
With an open hand he casually beckoned
'We'll play hide and seek' is what he reckoned
'I'll count to thirty' he sincerely said
'And a short time later you'll be dead'
'One' he said and got to four
And then you fled through an open door

Three minutes, four minutes absolute max
He's followed and reached the end of your tracks
He shouts 'Thirty seconds left to live'
'And then I'll strain your brain through a sieve'
Outside the door he stands in silence
The last few moments before the violence
One to ten tick tock you by

Alone in darkness you want to cry
'Thirteen... thirteen' whispered in low pitch
'I'm here for you to kill the witch'
Tap, tap, tap, on the door of the larder
Your heart races and pounds even harder
No rush, in a hush, hide and seek
With the next ten seconds blacker than bleak
You throw open the shield of the door
And scurry across the tiles of the floor
A fleeting glimpse of the hammer and chisel
And kitchen windows drenched in the drizzle
'Twenty-eight, twenty-nine, thirty... thirty!' he screams
'I'll see you in my world of dreams'
He laughs as you run even harder
Away from the tomb of the larder
'Run boy' he shouts 'hide and seek'
'But we both know we're the son of a freak'
Empty corridor, empty room
His idle laughter flows up the flume

Five minutes, six minutes absolute max
You escape by retracing the prints of your tracks
Back out into the murk of the drizzle
Still holding his hammer and chisel
Alone in the damp and the silence
The last few moments before the start of the violence
'Hide and seek' softly said
'And now it's time that you were dead'
Metal on bone hammered with a thud
On your cheeks a diluted river of blood
To your knees with only seconds to live
Tap, tap, tap, goes the chisel on sieve.

Trapped in the Black
666

I'm so alone, but there's no way back
If you can hear me, I'm trapped in the black
He came to see me, the uninvited guest
And with his scythe he crushed my chest
Then he mocked me with his slow hand clapping
As I lay there, my last breaths gasping

I fell from life to a place called dead
The lights went out, but my pneuma fled
If this is the norm I cannot tell
I'm not close to heaven, but near to hell
There's no ticking clock, no time to gauge
Is chronic isolation death's second stage?

I'm a fading picture of a random thought
A forgotten archive through which to sort
All that I am is an ethereal essence
A withering dream of a once real presence
And I'm so alone, but there's no way back
No one can hear me, I'm trapped in the black

All that I had went one by one
A last memory to purge and then I'll be gone
But it's him, with his slow hand clapping
And I'm lying there, my last breaths gasping
...clapping... gasping... the reaper is my keeper
...clapping... gasping... the reaper is my keeper
(ad infinitum)

Radioactive
666

Your aura shines bright, like it's radioactive
A glistening effusion much too attractive
My peri daydream my heart's in a clamour
And if we converse now I think I might stammer

I'm loathsomely rancid and sickly sallow
As you show me a card from your pack of tarot
My voluptuous vixen, or my vestal virgin
My blood is clotting and in need of purging

I'm a kaleidoscopic, cankerous, aberration
A malformed obscenity without affiliation
But here we are and here together
Trapped in a spell that could last forever

You're so winsome, with fair hair or blonde
And in your hazel eyes do I espy an inkling of a bond?
Your enigmatic smile is as sweet as sun-kissed honey
And melts my heart as my knees go feebly funny

If I could speak, I'd be slyly witty
Though your demeanour is that of one who is taking pity
But I'm here with you in this mute man's trance
As you deal the cards of fate, not fickle chance

And now your icy eyes shine bright, as if radioactive
With a mischievous glint that's not so attractive
My peri daydream you've abandoned your glamour
And in a dainty hand you now hold a hammer

I'm damp and pasty and sickly sallow
Short of breath and akin to callow
My voluptuous vixen, you're no vestal virgin
And there's no hope for me is what's emerging

I thought your smile was enigmatic
But now, with hindsight, I should've been pragmatic
'Cos between your ruby lips, what lies beneath
Are the hacksaw blades of your jagged teeth

I'll back away from your wretched grinning
'Cos in this situation I'll not be winning
My cloying blood is as thick as sun-kissed honey
Clogging arteries; my blurred vision sees nothing funny

And now I'm on the ground and you're astride
Though still voluptuous, I realize, you're another's bride
I'm your quarry, but we're here together
And I'm trapped in your spell, now and forever

I can't breathe and I'm sickly sallow
And the grave I'm in is much too shallow
You've ripped out my throat with your jagged teeth
And purged the cloying blood that lay beneath

Your aura shines bright, 'cos you're radioactive
And your gore filled smile is almost attractive
Now in my silent heart, gone is the clamour
As you raise the glistening claw of your hideous hammer.

Pseudo Superhuman

666

In the abandoned dreams of your defunct rhythm, delta
With your eyelids, post closure, a shuttered shelter
You're forsaking the flesh and purging a numen
The fictitious omnipresence of a pseudo superhuman

Now you're free and apart from all that was harming
And they're replacing your blood with the fluids of embalming
In contempt of eternity to life you faithfully clung
But now you're perfectly pickled, without a breath in a lung

From a toxic chalice you supped on aqua fortis
And now you're a waxen pose of rigor mortis
Your tower finally falling due to its corroded mortar
And now you're on marble, a leather sack for water

There's naught to see without cerebral function
No Elysian fields, no celestial junction
Your actuality was never a mystical rebus
And with inexistence there's no light from Phoebus

There's no chimera; there's no rhythm, delta
And your sealed eyelids are an empty shelter
Your incineration is a cremation of a numen
The fictitious omnipresence of a pseudo superhuman.

The Realm Of The Harlequin King

666

'Tis a dreamscape world of a misfiring mind
A fanciful vision of an improbable kind
Where spear-wielding picadors ride wild-eyed unicorns
Wearing fraudulent smiles and white leather uniforms
Abroad in the twilight lands, for their lord and master
The indomitable Harlequin King, the messiah of alabaster

In the ghoulish firmament of an ash-laden sky
The flesh-eating cormorant and vile vulture fly
Scouring the wastelands with a purposeful need
Seeking the rot of a corpse; to gorge on; to feed

'Tis a nightmare world of an ongoing battle
Fought by those bereft of credence or chattel
The faithless and zombies versus the chronically craven
Cannibal killers in a land without haven
A volcanic desolation with no songbird to sing
Just the wilds of the wilderness of the Harlequin King

In the oppressive firmament of an ash-laden sky
The flesh-eating cormorant and vile vulture spy
From the ramshackle ports by the salt sated sea
To the windswept calderas without refuge or lee

'Tis a delirious world of mayhem and fire
A cataclysmic vision where pure evil's the sire
A spent insipid sun sinks into a cankerous ocean
As skeletal herds roam in methodical motion
An army of shadows armed with cudgel and knife
Starved and diseased, with the rotten flesh rife

In his catacomb lair feasts the Harlequin King
Devouring fish of the sea and birds of the wing
He's absurdly debauched and away from what festers
Surrounded by sycophants and all his court jesters

'Tis a savage world of carnivorous creatures
Where they lost the faith and ate the preachers
Some found allegiance in the spurious spell
Of the anarchic clown borne from the bowels of hell
A covert tyrant, their lord and master
The post apocalyptic messiah of alabaster

On the black dust and rocks they clash and they kill
Cudgels and blades, heads off with a bill
To the victors the spoils of putrefied meat
And the eyes of the dead for a succulent treat

'Tis a dreamscape world of death and destruction
No wizards, just cannibals and the magma eruption
No god in the heavens, no white knights or leaders
Only the wretched, the wizened and the zombie flesh feeders
All raging with madness in their sickening war
From the high petrified lava to the sea-salted shore

Beneath the choking firmament of an ash-laden sky
The flesh-eating cormorant and vile vulture cry
They're ripping and stripping with talons and beaks
Devouring the carrion from stomachs and cheeks

'Tis a nightmare world of blood spilt in slaughter
Brutality, butchery and naught sought for quarter
Where the sword-bearing ranger rides the cadaverous horse
Wearing the white leather mask of his rampaging force
Wielding archaic justice with a dismembering swing
In the wilderness realm of the Harlequin King.

Telepaths

666

Hey! You can't fool me, I've done the math
There's more than one fucking telepath
He's one, she's one and so are you
Fuck you all and form a queue
Telepaths, telepaths, so many fucking telepaths
Transmitting messages with their cerebral telegraphs

You twist my thoughts in my grey matter splatter
Then feed off my ego and try to flatter
But you can kiss my ass and face my wrath
'Cos there's more than one fucking telepath
Hey, skull fucker, who are you?
I didn't see you in the fucking queue!

Telepaths, telepaths, a hundred fucking telepaths
I'm gonna crack my skull and let the contents drool
Transmitting messages with their cerebral telegraphs
And drain out my brain like it's fucking gruel
Telepaths, telepaths, a thousand fucking telepaths
Get out, fuck off, it's fucking cruel
Transmitting messages with their cerebral telegraphs

Hair and bone, my blood stains the bath
I'm purging more than one fucking telepath
I'm one, she's one and so are you
Fuck you all and join the queue
Telepaths, telepaths, so many fucking telepaths
Transmitting messages with their cerebral telegraphs

Have your say as I grey matter splatter
My head versus wall makes such a fucking clatter

Now you can kiss my ass, 'cos I've lost my wrath
I can't hear one fucking telepath
Hey, skull fuckers, I fucked you!
Fuck you all and fuck your queue

I'm cold and tingly; now I'm numb
The fucking telepaths have taken every crumb...

Treble Six

666

They dialled treble six and reversed the charge
Then took the piss and had it large
But Satan has no sense of humour
And that's a fact and not a rumour
How they goaded and took the mick
Told smutty jokes and called him thick
He listened carefully to their raucous laughter
And was mild and meek, like a well-trained actor

He clicked his claws upon the phone
Had delicious visions of bodies prone
Content and happy that they had dialled
If he could have, he would have smiled

They suggested he was a merchant banker
Was unforgiving and full of rancour
But Satan has no sense of guilt
And that's a fact of a stature built
How they taunted with jokes of reaper grim
Tried to mimic and called him dim
He listened carefully to their macho threats
Was mild and meek and made notes of debts

He saw their smug faces, almost gurning
Had delicious visions of their bodies burning
Content and happy with his heart of stone
He clicked his claws and hung up the phone

They had dialled treble six and reversed the charge
Then they took the piss and had it large
But Satan has no sense of humour
And that's a fact and not a rumour
So he rode forth on his black-as-night mare
And found the mockers and didn't spare
He gnashed and growled, like crazed with rabies
Pared their bodies and stole their babies

He clicked his claws whilst texting, SMS
'You got what you earned, no more, no less'
Content and happy he ceased his gorge
And what remained went to the forge

They foolishly dialled the number of the beast
And upon them he chose to feast
For bloody meat Satan has the flavour
And the flesh of man he'll especially savour
They no longer goad or take the mick
Tell smutty jokes or call him thick
He had listened carefully to their raucous laughter
And was briefly serene, like a well-trained actor.

Nyctophobia
666

You're drowning in the blackout's nothingness space
An essence of horror cruelly etched on your face
No effulgence for comfort, nothing glistens or glimmers

The angst that was buried now bubbles and simmers
Adrift and crestfallen in a delirium of dark
You're ensnared in the panic of a predicament stark

They're there, they creep, the spiders and rats
And the Devil's disciples armed with razors and bats
The cold of your sweat trickles and moistens
The spittle of your saliva is a mixture of poisons
Statuesque, froze in a pose, like a mannequin doll
Like you're awaiting the wield of an axe on a pole

Time passes... you push up and stumble across to a curtain
Pulling it open, black is the only thing certain
The tar that is night is consuming your breath
Squeezing out air to asphyxiate to death
You whimper, you shake, whilst shedding the tears
Knowing in the dark are your slithering fears

The fickle current reconnects to illuminate your space
Your blinking damp eyes look like they've tasted the Mace
A briefness of comfort, soothed by the glimmer
But the hundred watt bulb fades and falls dimmer
Reflected and framed he lours and looms
Trapped in the glass as you're plunged back to gloom

Only silence and stillness... no blade in your back
But all that exists is blacker than black
No streetlights, no moon, no twinkling of stars
Not even the passing headlights of cars
Beyond and within, either side of the curtain
The dark is a vortex, of that you are certain.

Snow White Dove

666

In his head she's as pure as a snow white dove
But a complicit purveyor of forbidden love
In her ruination there's a nook for him
And a sordid promise for the desirously grim

He feeds the lock of the old oak door
Within she waits, for him, he's sure
The creaks and groans of a rusty hinge
Resonate menacingly to make a madman cringe
In the turrets and towers of red brick walls
She's there, she wants, and like a siren calls
Below the crescent moon as the heavens glisten
He creeps in and holds his breath to listen
In a crusty pocket he secretes his keys
Then carefully hearkens to her seductive pleas
With his shadow cast by his lantern's light
He climbs the stairs of a well-known flight
Behind his back the oak door closes
As his power surges, like a new age Moses
She calls to pander and make him weaker
With his madman's smile he's her asylum seeker

In his head she holds a snow white dove
And sings a solemn song of forbidden love
If not wanton she'll still yield to him
And fulfil his needs so desirously grim

He quickly passes empty padded cells
A wicked grin and no alarming bells
He pants and sweats and licks his lips
On his chin the drool seeps then drips

Echoing down stone steps of a red brick tower
She calls to him without cause to cower
He feels the rage of his ravenous urge
Of what lies within he needs to purge
And then he's there, outside her door
Beyond which she waits for him, he's sure
The creaks and groans of a rusty hinge
Resonate menacingly to make a madman cringe
She's there in a corner, in his lantern's light
The physical remains of a vengeful wight
Behind his back the door grates and closes
As his power resurges, like a new age Moses

In his head she's a snow white dove
And a willing vendor of forbidden love
In her ruination there's a nook for him
And a sordid promise for the desirously grim

All his needs are base and vicious
But now his screams are so delicious
She feeds the desecration of his fire
Then shreds his body with his razor wire
She called, he wanted, he came to meet
But her brutal vengeance was honey sweet
A foam of spittle upon his butchered lips
On his chin the blood seeps then drips
In the turrets and towers of red brick walls
There's solace in silence and no siren calls
From the highest parapet flies a snow white dove
Now purged of hate and in search of love
Under a crescent moon, if the heavens glisten
You might hear his horror, if you carefully listen
In her padded cell his death was dire
Wrapped and shredded in his razor wire.

The Pagan Heist

666

A pagan ritual, a midwinter heist
All in the name of Jesus Christ
Part the waters like Jehovah Moses
Or spread the bullshit on your wilting roses

Abraham's children and promised lands
All straw castles built on shifting sands
Holy wars and self-righteous preservation
Two thousand years of ordained decimation

The Jesus ritual, midwinter heist
All for naught with a pagan Christ
Someone part the waters like Jehovah Moses
And show us the miracles of the ancient proses

Pray to the ether on your bended knees
Then carve your symbols from rocks and trees
Holy wars and self-righteous preservation
Twenty centuries of ordained desecration

A pagan ritual for Jesus Christ
A confirmed conversion in a midwinter heist
There's no need to escape through parted waters
'Cos we've got guns and bombs and holy mortars

Brothers, sisters and mother fuckers
Let's put our heads in gas filled cookers
The flaming cross, star and the crescent
Die in the past; live in the present.

We Burned Together

666

We burned together in nuclear pyres
Continents, states and all of the shires
We sought a solution fatally unflawed
With the self-incineration of our hungering horde

We were apathetically incurable and utterly dire
The blind leading the deluded into a fathomless mire
We took what we wanted with omnivorous greed
The fat cats and feeders with an insatiable need

We burned together in nuclear fires
The mad, the bad and the sanctimonious liars
Gone the government crooks; the alliance of churches
And the psychotic fascists brandishing birches

In our desperate death throes we begged to our gods
But they replied with a blight and lightning to rods
So we sought our solace in a vengeful notion
We'd scorch the earth and boil the ocean

So it was we were consumed in the plume of the fire
Razing synagogue, mosque and every church spire
On the oily surface of a precipitous bevel
We slipped off the edge and soon met the Devil

We burned together in nuclear pyres
The imams; the rabbis; the farcical priors
We sought a solution for omnivorous greed
With the self-incineration of our troublesome breed.

The Devil's Spawn

666

Not from the loins of man, but a devil's spawn
She was created, from no seed born
Salacious, rapacious, an imp called Vera
And what she wanted could not be clearer

No need for the stick when I saw the carrot
She kissed my neck to taste the claret
No bite of love, just her hunger pangs
As she gouged and gorged with carnivorous fangs

A small price to pay to quench the lust
For the needful flesh with grind and thrust
Nails for nails, Vera was a manic shredder
Diffusing blood as if through a spreader

Always in control, I knew her ruse
As I poisoned her with noxious juice
She filled till sated like I was tapped to broth
But she paid the price with a toxic froth

Not from the loins of man, but the Devil's spawn
Maybe I was created, from no seed born
Salacious, rapacious, akin to the imp Vera
And what I wanted could not be clearer

Though ailing she still gorged with no compulsion
As I fed my needs without revulsion
She grew weaker, as I grew stronger
Till her rotting flesh I could stand no longer

For the grand finale she saved the best
Hammering a stake into my chest
Sweet devilish child you've played your part
But my blood is poison and I have no heart

Now in my arms she lies here limp
The naked body of the former Vera imp
When you live forever and are lord of flies
You can pick and choose who lives, who dies.

Dead by Dawn
666

Deep in your sleep in the dark of the wood
Where lunar beams creep through branches in bud
The muntjac's at rest, the badger's at play
With the rook and the raven holding sway till the day

Fragrantly sweet is the succulent air
Barefooted you wander without a thought or a care
Merrily gambolling in your idyll-like haven
But they're watching together, the rook and the raven

Asleep in a bed there's an REM flicker
Past 3 am and a heart pounds a beat quicker
Living a dream time haggard and worn
Rouse and awake before night turns to dawn

Cataract motes glitter amongst branches
The canopy top is soaked till it blanches
Apathetic and bloated is the ominous moon
With first light approaching at an hour that's soon

Deep in your sleep in the dark of the wood
Where the calmness of peace is in situ with good
The muntjac's in cover, the badger is plagued
By the rook and the raven who are stubbornly staid

There's a carpet of flowers the colour of heather
Covering the ground that's as soft as a feather
You merrily meander by a babbling brook
Intently observed by the raven and rook

Asleep in a bed there's an REM flicker
Past 4am and a heart pounds another beat quicker
Living a dream time haggard and worn
Walk to the light before night turns to dawn

You imbibe from the waters, the taste is appealing
Honey-sweet nectar infused with warm feeling
A gulp and a swallow, a handful to pour
Never quite sated, just a little bit more

Disguise and take flight to escape what is real
Evading the carnage and closing the deal
Assuaging your want by taking the bait
Delirium aspires to be your festering fate

Below the full moon, in the darkest of hours
You'll burn and you'll fade like meteor showers

Desire aspires to be your intimate trait
Appeasing your fear, but feeding your hate
Will o' the wisp, willingly led
Nothing in dreams, but endowing the dead

Too deep in your sleep in the gloom of the wood
First beams of the sun creep through branches in bud
The muntjac has roved, the badger will stay
With the rook and the raven holding sway through the day

Pungently sweet is the odorous air
You lie by the brook without a thought or a care
Dragging in breaths in your idyll-like haven
But they're watching together, the rook and the raven

Unconscious in bed there isn't a flicker
Past 5 am the blood seeps through the ticker
Living a nightmare time haggard and worn
You stayed with the dark when night turned to dawn

Cataract motes filter through branches
The canopy top is heated till it blanches
Raging and bloated is the ominous sun
Daylight arrives and there's nowhere to run

Succumbed in your sleep, your heart's in the wood
Where death and decay are in situ with good
The muntjac's in clover, the badger lies slayed
With the rook and the raven still stubbornly staid

There's a carpet of flowers as prickly as heather
Covering the ground that's as hard as old leather
Quietly you fade by the babbling brook
Intently observed by the raven and the rook

Lifeless in bed, there isn't a flicker
Past 6 am there's not a beat from the ticker
The dream was a nightmare time haggard and worn
You went with the dark when night turned to dawn

The rook and the raven find a taste that's appealing
Honey-sweet meat infused with warm feeling
They gouge and they swallow and take a little bit more
Till they are sated and bloated, of that they are sure.

Zombie

666

He's a zombie; he has a fixed, crazed, stare
Pockmarked skin and clippers cropped hair
And a humourless grin, that's barely a smile
That turns my stomach till I taste the bile

I can feel his rage, he wants to right some wrongs
But his manic verbiage is in a dead man's tongues
He taps his head and then his finger's pointing
Straight at me, like I need anointing

I can smell the carrion of putrefied meat
A stagnant odour close to sickly sweet
If I could I'd like to gag, not swallow
And purge my guts and leave them hollow

He's a zombie; his sensibility's shorn
And I can feel the ire in his incandescent scorn
He's up to the brink and I'm closed in a hem
As I spit out a tooth and a globule of phlegm

There's a voice in my cranium, amongst all that's dull
'Your zombie friend's gonna smash your skull'
In my sanity there are some hairline cracks
But in a moment of clarity I can see his axe

I can feel his rage, he wants to right some wrongs
So I try to placate in his dead man's tongues
But he's the judge and jury of the self-appointing
Another tap of the head and his finger's pointing

He was a zombie; till I ripped off his head

Then I ate his brain, like it was buttered bread
There are holes in my cheeks and I've lost three fingers
And my stagnant odour cloys as it lingers

There's a voice in my cranium, amongst all that's dull
'Rip out his guts, now that you've drained his skull'
In my sanity there's a major faultline crack
'Cos I've split open his stomach and intestinal sac

I can feel the warmth of his internal heat
And there's a fetid stench close to sickly sweet
I try not to gag as I chew and swallow
But with a rancid reflux I purge till hollow

I'm a zombie; with a fixed, crazed, stare
Sallow skin and sweat drenched hair
With a ghastly grin, that's barely a smile
I can feel the acid burn as I taste the bile.

A Cupid Stunt

666

A smile, a pout and a little wink
What the fuck was I s'posed to think?
She was the inferno burning my wood
But the fire was a pyre fuelled by a scud
With a blind man's hunch I took a punt
But she was nothing more than a cupid stunt

She had devilish desires, I had an uncontrollable rise
When she ground me down between her highly toned thighs
And there was a simmering sneer upon her luscious lips
As she pinned me down beneath her grinding hips

I had looked for love, but the moment was fleeting
'Cos she rode me hard and gave me a beating

I thought she was a crazy horse and its rider
But she was a fucking evil black widow spider
She took my semen, then blood in gallons
As she dug and raked with her fucking talons
To that fucking bitch I took affront
'Cos I got fucking battered due to a cupid stunt

To her sadistic pleasures I wasn't wise
Till she tried to gouge out my fucking eyes
I punched her face and those luscious lips
And thrust a knee up to her grinding hips
But she cracked my skull with a spherical ornament
As I found myself in a gladiatorial tournament

Now I can't smile, but I twitch and blink
'Cos she caved my head in, so I can't think
She fucking chewed me, like a cow with cud
And fucking left me in a pool of blood
But I laughed last with her implement blunt
Stopped her dead and stopped a cupid stunt.

Felo De Se

666

Clocks will stop and their ticks and tocks
Unnoticed we'll fade, with Fermi's paradox
Destroying the myths from Alpha to Omega
No ascension to heaven for any believer

Self-imploding, with nowhere to run
No escaping from the third rock from the sun
The non-intelligent and the AI mainframe
Have it planned, all the way to the endgame

Clocks will stop and their ticks and tocks
We'll be forever lost, with Fermi's paradox
Gone the delusions of pandemic insanity
And the idle threat of the singularity

Fires will burn, like the Devil's furnace
Evaporating sweat, searing epidermis
Levelling the conurbation and the tundra
Obscuring the sky with a noxious umbra

Dantean daydreams might arise tomorrow
Existing today, from the pro tem we'll borrow
Smell now the smoke from the fated flames
Erasing the crops, all the seeds and the grains

Clocks will stop and their ticks and tocks
As we violently vanish, with Fermi's paradox
Gone the verdant fields of sun-kissed grasses
Under a toxic sky of smouldering ashes

There'll be nowhere to hide, nowhere to run
No reverence paid to the third rock of the sun
The non-intelligent and the AI mainframe
Will play it out, all the way to the endgame

Clocks will stop and their ticks and tocks
As we die alone, with Fermi's paradox
Destroying the myths and the grand illusion
Nurtured from the seeds of self-delusion

Perfect Wars

666

Only balanced books will pay the piper
To call the tune we'll curb the sniper...
In imprudent conflicts there is an angst
With open warfare with foot and tanks
No guns, no bombs, no blood letting
There'll be a chosen few found through vetting

There'll come the day when we fight our wars
In covert sanctuaries behind locked doors
In dorms and hangars, strapped to couches
Web wired and plumbed to fluid pouches
Elite cohorts aligned on floors
Dreamscape fighters of a noble cause
In red light auras, in different slouches
With clipboard prefects in silent crouches

We'll find common sense in our neurosis
Deranged involvement in our psychosis
No smoking ruins of collateral damage
Economic glee for those who manage

Silent combat, with silent foes
Carnage free and no death throes

There'll come the day when we pay the debt
Thanks to the cannon fodder trapped in the net
When the napalm burns they'll feel no pain
With a humane injection into a vein
Black ops soldier, ace in a jet
In exploding pixels their fates are met
No VCs for the fried insane
Bagged on trollies for those deemed slain

In our perfect world we'll fight perfect wars
In covert sanctuaries behind locked doors
Quiet conflicts, whilst strapped to couches
With clipboard prefects in silent crouches...
Only cash in hand will pay the piper
To call the tune we'll watch the sniper.

Black Flags

666

Their black flags fluttered with cross and crescent
As they gathered all from lord to peasant
With sharpened blades they teased our tongues
And held before us barbed metal prongs

In our faces they waved their holy books
Demented eyes and full crazed looks
We were stretched on racks below crumbling spires
As they scorched our flesh with their raging fires

How I screamed, before my sins confessed
They stripped me bare and then redressed
For their mercy granted I pledged allegiance
And now I serve with blind obedience

We seek our strength in gushing rants
Prayers for guidance and submissive chants
Black flags with crescents and Christian crosses
Rippling as we hunt in righteous posses

Only liberating pain can redeem the liars
For those uncleansed will burn on pyres
Between heaven and hell they'll be brought to yield
Saved by suffering under our protective shield

In their faces we wave our holy books
Tormented eyes and half crazed looks
They're stretched on racks below ruined spires
On their flesh the cinders from our raging fires

How they scream, before their sins confessed
They plead, implore, with faith protest
Some beg of God, others call to Allah
Odin's children will find Valhalla

From their mouths we cut their tongues
And cook till tender on metal prongs
The sinners silenced as they profusely bleed
Before, with mercy, we despatch with speed

Only lingering death can redeem the liars
As we burn their bodies on holy pyres
We saved their souls in blood soaked fields
Then cleaned our blades and raised our shields

We take our strength from the blessed book
Finding guidance to the heathens nook
The cross in crescent on black flags flutter
As we hunt to purge the tainted clutter.

This Midnight Hour

666

This time that's now, this midnight hour
Hiding those who creep and lour
Inside your mind, they're in your head
Sneakily slithering towards your bed

Mark the time and feel what's present
In the black below the lifeless crescent
Dire is the darkness as they slyly slink
Not close yet, but nearer than you think
In disturbing dreams do you soundly sleep?
Gnashing teeth ward off those who creep
Hideous creatures who skulk and lour
Take their advantage in this midnight hour

Heinous Harpies with sharpened claws
Outside your head, but inside your doors
Unconscious dreamer can you feel them sink
Rapacious fangs into you, the gink?

ECT

(Electroconvulsive Torture)

666

They fried my brains with their electric shocks
And switched my mind from ticks to tocks
And though intensely keen they wanted no reportage
But in volts and amps they had no shortage

Seth said to Cedric 'Let's show him heaven'
Then turned the dial up to eleven
They tried to macerate my cerebral cortex
And send my brain cells into a black hole vortex

I used to tick, but now I tock
After they fed me their electric shock
They fucked my body and fried my head
But now those pricks are fucking dead

I was bound with straps, the couch was shaking
As through my temples I was current taking
Bulging eyes and Adam's apple
And locked like rock in a seizure grapple

Seth said to Cedric 'Let's cook him good'
'And turn his brains into charcoal wood'
All that voltage caused the lights to flicker
Burned my flesh and ripped my ticker

I used to tick, but now I tock
After the voltage of their electric shock
They fucked my body and fried my head
But now those rimmers are fucking dead

Like a fat fuck who's much too pursy
I sucked in air when they showed some mercy
Down came the amps and I broke my shackles
Then grabbed them both by their wedding tackles

I was crazed, I was smokin'
Seth and Cedric, in pain, were chokin'
I squeezed their balls, then ripped to shreds
Then between my blackened hands I crushed their heads

I no longer tick, but I fucking tock
And for Seth and Cedric it was a fucking shock
They tried hard to fry my cerebral cortex
But I sent those rimmers into a black hole vortex.

New Eden Garden

666

With their rapturous epiphany all our troubles were gone
As all the Abrahamic disciples united as one
And when the heavens were illuminated with a meteor shower
'Twas a sign of divinity, a blossoming ascendancy flower

Assuaged and reaffiliated with the guidance of His hand
He then spoke to them of a realignment planned
So they profusely effervesced of a new Eden garden
Where the blasphemous pagans might be accorded a pardon

All the manic ministers and priggish preachers
With the euphoric eyes of rhapsodic teachers
Endorsed and empowered, all stoned on felonious bongs
Hatched their plans in garrulous, drug-fuelled tongues

They ruled with an iron fist across every nation
Cleansed those unfit with flagellation
Called for our prayers on a daily basis
And fed the supplicants; empty minds; empty faces

In the mounting oppression there was unrest and resistance
With some even claiming His non-existence
But they fooled us with their promise of a new world order
Fair, famine free and banned, the hoarder

They were crazed on crack cocaine and crystal meth
When He ordained them with His warrant of death
And then He showed them their new Eden Garden
For the unctuous meek who bore no sin for a pardon

The chosen few, with poker faces and royal flushes
Tripped in flights of fancy as they talked to burning bushes
And with His utopian gift they were delighted
All the Abrahamic disciples, as one, united

Thus the heavens were illuminated with a nuclear shower
A divine intervention of the ultimate power
With their ICBMs and their stock of toxic gases
They nullified all the ignorant, faithless, masses

Once alone in the wasteland of their New Eden Garden
They sought for His solace and begged for His pardon
And with their collective conscience they tried to wrestle
Whilst drawing in holy smoke from a bubbling vessel

All the manic ministers and priggish preachers
With the euphoric eyes of rhapsodic teachers
Were crazed on crack cocaine and crystal meth
When they ordained their own sanctimonious death

They called for our prayers on a daily basis
But laid waste to the lands and all of the races
They slaughtered us all and now everything has gone
All the Abrahamic disciples, every innocent one.

We are the Ghosts

666

We are the living and we are the ghosts
Ethereal essences, guests of physical hosts
Alive and alight, with our deaths to follow
Resonating in time we'll haunt the morrow
Enveloped in flesh our encompassed somatic
Takes limited paths, prosaically pragmatic
Hastened by time we'll be as one with the daisies
Entering the mysterious realm of Heaven and Hades
Gone and forgotten, we'll resonate the morrow
Haunting the living, but unable to follow
Ours was the corporeal and now the hereafter
Sometimes you'll sense our echoing laughter
Taken from the living, now we are the ghosts
Shadowy shapes without physical hosts.

The Black Castle

666

He can smell the sea salt and sense the motion
Of the crashing waves of the deepest ocean
Whipped to a crescendo by the winds tumultuous howling
That covers the footsteps of those out prowling

He disperses the shadows with a burning candle
But each night they return to try the handle

Outside they hiss and snigger and often mock
As they tease, with a key, his fastened lock

He lies there, frightened, on the stone-flagged floor
As they scrape, with their claws, down the cell's oak door
And each time they'll whisper a chilling warning
'Your light will fade before the break of morning'

And then they'll move on; on to another's cell
Where the candle's faded and they're dragged to hell
With forlorn screams they plunge to the molten mire
Into the fiery furnace of the Devil's shire

Here starts hell, inside the baleful black castle
It's a harrowing place and a Hades state vassal
Shifting shadows seek the maudlin mourners
Fetus formed and curled up in dingy corners
Ocean storms cannot flood the portal
Rampaging waves cannot save the mortal
Hell awaits through the gates and the gates are open
Extracting the souls of the conned and the broken
Light fades fast to black with a withering wick
Loosening a lock that will turn with a click

High in a desolate cell of the fortified rock
He's alone in the dark and there's a key in the lock
The shadows converged with the wane of the candle
With a grate and a creak they're turning the handle

He's curled in a corner, on the flags of the floor
The key has been turned and they're opening the door
And how he wishes for the poison of a potion
Or to be drowning himself in the waves of the ocean

And now they're in; they're in his cell
The red reptilian eyes of those born in hell
His final screams are ones of wretched anguish
For in the fiery furnace he's about to languish

It's just the wind and not a fallen soul's pitiful howl
And that was shifting timbers and not reptilians on the prowl
But in your dreams there's a persistent warning
'Your light will fade before the break of morning.'

So Many Voices

666

So many voices, all turning the screw
Outside, inside, I haven't a clue

Malignant murmurings are borne from my mania
Asking questions of your schizophrenia
Nagging doubts are a poisonous potion
You, them and I all bereft of emotion

Voices, voices, all those vehement voices
Outside, inside, I'm spoilt for choices
I sought my id, but found your egos
Covertly flourishing like a well-fed tree grows
Elusive personae haven't a clue
So many voices, all turning the screw.

One Eye Blind

666

Ghouls and demons and vampires too
All dropping acid and sniffing glue
They're crazed like fuck and completely manic
On the streets there's a fucking panic

Off their heads; the sweat is dripping
No one's safe when they're fucking tripping
They're in moonlight shadows of the park and alley
Where they'll feed on those who choose to dally

Locks on windows, bolts on doors
Distract yourselves with menial chores
When they're out of sight, you're in your mind
So turn your back and one eye blind

Ghouls and demons who are dropping acid
Hunt to kill, 'cos their cocks are flaccid
Vicious vampires always cause a ruckus
When supping blood, they're mother fuckers

Can you hear the screams of some poor runt
Trapped and butchered in the fuckers' hunt?
Or is the white noise static so overpowering
That with your one eye blind you'll not be cowering?

They drag their victims into drainage ditches
Given time they'd cull the witches
Casting spells with tongue of toad
Won't curse the fuckers, but merely goad

Ghouls and demons all crazed to fuck
Will seek their victims in niche and nook
And beware the vampire when he's fucking tripping
He'll devour you like you were toast and dripping

Call to Jesus and find your crosses
But in the opaque moonlight you'll still suffer losses
In the blackest shadows they'll sate their wrath
And immerse and bathe you in your own blood bath

Fuck the ghoul, fuck the demon
Who spread their plague like rancid semen
Hammer a stake into a vampires heart
Then pop his eyes with a silver dart...

...Or, turn a deaf ear and one eye blind
But they're outside your door, I think you'll find
They're smackhead crazy, they're fucking manic
And now it's time for you to panic.

Your Bloody Hands

666

Your bloody hands remind you and taunt you
They're still stained, they're blemished to haunt you
They killed him and you killed the clown
With his hideous greasepainted frown

Your bloody hands did what they did
Took the switchblade and did what you bid
A pool of blood and you had bloody hands
Because they executed one of your murderous plans

Your bloody hands wrapped him; wrapped him in tarps
Then dug a shallow grave and buried his corpse
His death mask was a red nose and a smile
Contrary to your intent of homicidal guile

Your bloody hands remind you and taunt you
They're still stained, they're blemished to haunt you
They took his boots and his wig, they took his crown
Left him with his bloody nose and greasepainted frown

Your bloody hands did what they did
Took the switchblade and did what you bid
But killed clowns, from the dead, they will rise
And come back and look into their murderers' eyes

You know he'll find you, to remind you of what you did
And then he'll hack them off, those that did what you bid
His maggoty hands will come back to taunt you
But your bloody hands will no longer haunt you.

Slipknot

666

And there it was, just dangling free
From the thickest branch of an old oak tree
In pristine condition; a melancholic mystery
Like an ornament left from a dark day in history

Amongst the undergrowth he espied and found
A half-concealed log upon the ground
And upon its rotten wood he carefully put
The searching sole of a booted foot

Above his head he could feel its prickly presence
Seducing him into a calamitous coalescence
Tempting the tainted; looking for a weak spot
The loop of the noose, the snare of the slipknot

Somewhere in his jumbled thoughts he knew he could
Place both feet upon that rotten wood
And so there he was, having lost his thread
As malevolent rope-work teased his sweating head

Summer's distant birdsong was the background noise
As upon that log he balanced with a certain poise
In an oppression of heat, that was close to searing
He stood alone, off the track of a woodland clearing

In his hands he could feel its prickly presence
Their fates now entwined in a ghastly coalescence
Then it was around his neck; around his weak spot
The loop of the noose, the snare of the slipknot

Snap; the log cracked and crumbled
Lynching him as he grasped and tumbled
In the air, six inches from the ground
Panic stricken, feeling his every pound

Kicking and gasping in a death throes choke
Noosed from the thickest branch of a woodland oak
Oesophagus and trachea, it had found his weak spot
The loop of the noose, the slide of the slipknot

And there he hangs, just dangling free
Gently swaying below an old oak tree
He's gone, he's passed, he's on the other side
Cajoled into the snare of a slipknot suicide.

Vampire Hunters

666

We wear a mask and cape; head in a hood
When we're hunting vampires for their meat and blood
Garottes, cut-throat razors and our glistening claws
Take care of the pretty boys and their sidekick whores

In the empty pre-dawn's low wattage light
We'll covertly wait beyond their night vision sight
They're puerilely predictable, with set times to feed
But when we catch them we'll dispatch with speed

Sometimes we'll chase, then kill with silver bullets
Then suck out their brains and rip out their gullets
For a savoury snack we'll spit roast their livers
Iron rich and served in luscious slivers

Those pretty boy vampires who romance and court
Are our favourites and we'll hunt for sport
We'll trap and snare them and wait for the sun
If they beg for mercy we might load a gun

They can try, but they can't pierce our reptilian skins
They can try, but they can't escape our fang filled grins
We're vampire hunters, we're specialist boffins
We'll chase to kill, or wait by their coffins

We wear a mask and cape; head in a hood
When we butcher them for their meat and blood
They're not our creed, they're loathsome lazars
Who we dispatch with garottes and cut-throat razors.

It Creeps

666

Psst... Death; it creeps, yeah? And it creeps
It can slither, it can sidle
But it mostly creeps... and never sleeps
With a relentless flow you cannot bridle

Another beat, another breath
For what you have there is a debt
Its guise the scythe, it's your death
Think it through, dab the sweat

Death; it creeps, yeah? And it creeps
In the shifting shadows of enfeebling fear
In dreams it creeps... and never sleeps
In your dark, it's a shark, shed a tear

Aberrant beat, catch a breath
Now you'll focus on the debt
The price for life is your death
Think it through, dab the sweat

Death; it creeps, yeah? And it creeps
It can slither, it can sidle
Sets its net, as it creeps... and never sleeps
Always flows, never stops, is never idle

A flaccid beat, a laboured breath
What you'll lose will pay the debt
Here comes the scythe in search of death
Think it through, dab the sweat

Psst... Death; it creeps, yeah? And it creeps
For what is owed is overdue
A floorboard creaks, it never sleeps
And now it's here... it's come for you...

...gotcha...

The Word of Man

666

With reasoned thought I have concluded
That all their prophets were self-deluded
They sought not a deity, but the Word of Man
To construct their own self-serving master plan

Their sacred scriptures are works of fiction
Causing angst and ire; with rivals, friction
Now the pietistic think they're saving souls
As they wend their way like trawling trolls

Their self-scribed laws are all outdated
And to enlightened times are unrelated
Prayers and confessions, some choose to fast
Obeying conjured words born in the past

In their fancy dreams of make-believe
They snare the hapless and those naive
With no rational thoughts found in deliberation
Some regurgitate the prose of a unique Creation

All that came to fruition from the OT Bible
Divides the world and makes it tribal
A deity's words would leave no confusion
And in need of rewrites of opaque elocution

There's no god almighty, I have concluded
And I'll not doff my hat to the self-deluded
They searched in reveries and found the Word of Man
And constructed their own self-serving master plan.

H is for Hell!

666

D is the letter, D is for door
He sweats as he frets, does he know what it's for?
The maelstrom of his mind is too fucking fuzzy
As he mews,like a cat, a sad passive pussy
A push and a prod and he utters a mutter
He thinks he his sane, but is he a nutter?
He says 'It begins with a D, I think it's a door'
'And I'm sure that I know what the fuck it is for'
There's nothing to pull, he's caressing the metal
As his face fills up red and is as hot as a kettle
He's beleaguered, fatigued and well past his prime
And now he's beached on a door like a semi-crazed mime

'D' he whimpers 'D is for door'
Then... eureka!; a glowing disc, he knows what it's for
He presses it hard, he presses the button
Feeling bewildered with his thick head of mutton
A sideways retraction, no pull or a push
As he feels the flood of a full fucking blush
He staggers inside and he utters a mutter
He's probably not sane, but is he a nutter?
He says 'Don't stare at me, I'm as mad as a dog'
'And I'll punch out your lights, you Neanderthal trog'
It's him, there in the mirror, on the elevator wall
But he's wired, if not crazy and too fucking tall

It rattles, it's closing, the baffling door
He espies all the buttons, G and H, 1 up to 4
He sweats as he frets, he's so fucking nervous
As a celestial voice says 'This lift's out of service'
G is the letter for god, ground or gnome
And H is for heaven, or just the way home
He presses it hard, he presses the button
Feeling bewildered with his thick head of mutton
He's touching the cloth, he's plunging, he's falling!
The look on his face is truly appalling
'Fucking H!' he screams 'H is for hell!'
He hurtles to the bottom and ping goes the bell.